Martin Gicharu

The Efficacy of a Robust Church Leadership

Martin Gicharu

The Efficacy of a Robust Church Leadership

The need for skilful and adept leadership

Blessed Hope Publishing

Imprint

Cover image: www.ingimage.com

Publisher:
Blessed Hope Publishing
is a trademark of
Dodo Books Indian Ocean Ltd. and OmniScriptum S.R.L publishing group

120 High Road, East Finchley, London, N2 9ED, United Kingdom
Str. Armeneasca 28/1, office 1, Chisinau MD-2012, Republic of Moldova, Europe
Printed at: see last page
ISBN: 978-620-4-18827-0

THE EFFICACY OF A ROBUST CHURCH LEADERSHIP.

BY MARTIN GICHARU

Dedication.

I joyfully dedicate this work to all church leaders in the Body of Christ.

Everything rises and falls on the shoulders of a leader. Be a skillful leader and the church will realize a consequential increase.

Acknowledgement.

I express my indescribable joy and genuine gratitude to the Almighty God, in whom I have my being and the source of my life.

Secondly, I acknowledge my mentors who have been a bolster in my ministry, my father in faith, Bishop Dr. David Macharia, the General Overseer Full Gospel Churches of Kenya, Bishop Samuel Gitu, Central Rift Region Overseer and Bishop Alfred Kagiri, Nakuru Central District Overseer.

Special salutation to my brothers and sisters for their continued support in the ministry and for financial aid, may you never lack.

Contents

Introduction

Efficacy is the power to produce effect, the ability to exert influence, to instigate change and requires a leader who is robust, that is a person who is resilient and reliable, capable of consistently functioning at an optimal level under diverse circumstances, without experiencing the slightest hint of failure. Leadership can be defined as the ability of an individual or a group of people to influence and guide followers or members of an organization, society or team toward a desired direction or goal. This entails a set of behaviors used to help people align their collective direction, execute strategic plans through teamwork, and to continually achieve something new and better. Usually, the group leader is the vision-bearer and often takes risks and challenges the status quo to enable the fulfillment of the vision.

Leadership in any group is so crucial that it could be a leading factor in determining a group's ability to succeed and conquer against their enemy. Alexander the Great summarized this when he declared, "I am not afraid of an army of lions led by a sheep; I am afraid of an army of sheep led by a lion."

As in the case of many (if not all) other positions in a team or church, leadership can be good or bad depending on various characteristics. While good leadership is empowering and contributes to a team's success, bad leadership is a cause of failure and hurt in any team/group.

We will discuss various leadership models and theories to expound on the characteristics of good leadership in the next section but first, let's look at how to identify bad leadership. Some of the attributes of bad leadership include: lack of vision, ineffective or no communication, lack of accountability, selfishness, lack of accountability,

There's bad and good leadership?

Benefits/Roles of leadership in the church

In the church setting, the Holy Spirit and the Word of God are the ultimate sources of church leadership. However, it is biblical that God chooses specific persons to lead his people through a journey or towards achieving a goal. The leader provides sound advice, models godliness, and intercedes for the people of God, among other responsibilities.

In the church today, leadership is essential to providing and establishing:

1. Guidance and Direction: Leadership provides guidance and direction to the church community, helping to establish a clear vision, mission, and goals. Leaders help articulate the purpose of the ministry and provide a roadmap for its members to follow.

2. Spiritual Growth and Discipleship: Church leaders play a vital role in nurturing the spiritual growth and discipleship of individuals within the congregation. They provide teaching, mentorship, and pastoral care, helping individuals deepen their faith and develop a closer relationship with God.

3. Organizational Management: Effective leadership ensures the smooth functioning and efficient management of the church ministry. Leaders oversee various aspects, such as budgeting, resource allocation, program planning, and volunteer coordination, to ensure the ministry operates effectively and meets the needs of its members.

4. Community Building: Leaders foster a sense of community and belonging within the church. They create opportunities for fellowship, encourage meaningful relationships, and promote a

culture of inclusivity and support. This helps to strengthen the bonds among church members and create a welcoming environment for newcomers.

5. Outreach and Mission: Church leaders play a vital role in leading the ministry's outreach efforts and mission activities. They inspire and mobilize the congregation to engage in acts of service, evangelism, and social justice initiatives, both within the church community and in the wider society.

6. Stewardship and Accountability: Leaders are responsible for stewarding the resources, both financial and human, entrusted to the church ministry. They ensure transparency, accountability, and wise decision-making in managing these resources for the benefit of the congregation and the fulfillment of the ministry's mission.

7. Crisis Management and Support: In times of crisis or challenging situations, leaders provide support, comfort, and guidance to the church community. They offer pastoral care, prayer, and practical assistance, helping individuals navigate difficult circumstances and find hope and healing.

Overall, understanding and having effective leadership within a church ministry is essential for fostering spiritual growth, providing guidance, building community, and fulfilling the mission and purpose of the church.

Foundations of Leadership

There are different leadership theories and models that explore the key skills and behaviors that are essential for good effective leadership. Examples include:

Transformational Leadership:

Transformational leadership theory emphasizes the leader's ability to inspire and motivate followers to achieve higher levels of performance and personal growth. It was first introduced by James V. Downton in 1973 and further developed by James MacGregor Burns in 1978.

According to the theory, transformational leaders are characterized by their ability to create a vision, communicate it effectively, and inspire their followers to share and work towards that vision. They exhibit certain key behaviors that have a transformative impact on their followers. These behaviors include:

a. Idealized Influence: Transformational leaders serve as role models and gain the trust and respect of their followers through their ethical behavior, integrity, and high moral standards.
b. Inspirational Motivation: They inspire and motivate their followers by setting high expectations, articulating a compelling vision, and providing a sense of purpose and meaning in their work.
c. Intellectual Stimulation: Transformational leaders encourage creativity, innovation, and critical thinking among their followers. They challenge the status quo, promote intellectual curiosity, and foster an environment that values learning and growth.
d. Individualized Consideration: They demonstrate genuine concern for the individual needs, aspirations, and development of their followers. Transformational leaders provide support, mentorship, and personalized guidance to help their followers reach their full potential.

The ultimate goal of transformational leadership is to create positive change and transformation within individuals and organizations. By inspiring and empowering their followers, transformational leaders aim to achieve higher levels of performance, commitment, and satisfaction.

In the context of church ministry, transformational leaders inspire congregants by articulating a compelling vision, fostering a sense of purpose, and promoting spiritual growth and development.

It is important to note that although the theory of transformational leadership has been widely studied and applied in various contexts over the years, it still suffers its criticisms and limitations. Some of the limitations include:

1. Idealized Influence can lead to the idealization of leaders, potentially creating a dependency on them. This can hinder the development of independent thinking and decision-making among the group or church. In the church, this can sometimes be questioned or appear as idolatry.

2. Lack of Empirical Evidence: Critics argue that the empirical evidence supporting the effectiveness of transformational leadership is not always consistent. Some studies have shown positive outcomes, while others have found limited or no significant effects. This inconsistency raises questions about the generalizability and reliability of the theory.

3. Potential for Manipulation: Transformational leaders have the ability to inspire and motivate followers towards a shared vision. However, critics argue that this influence can be used manipulatively, potentially leading to the exploitation of followers' trust and loyalty. Indeed, this has been evident in some cults where the leaders manipulate and mislead followers. An example

here in Kenya is the “Shakahola” saga that saw hundreds if not thousands of Kenyans lose their lives this year.

4. Overemphasis on Charismatic Leadership: Transformational leadership theory often emphasizes the charismatic qualities of leaders, such as their ability to inspire and influence others. Critics argue that this focus on charisma may overlook other important leadership qualities, such as humility, empathy, and ethical decision-making.

5. Contextual Factors: Critics highlight the importance of considering contextual factors when applying transformational leadership theory. The effectiveness of transformational leadership may vary depending on the organizational culture, industry, and followers' characteristics. Failing to consider these contextual factors may limit the applicability of the theory.

6. Potential for Burnout: Transformational leaders are often highly engaged and invested in their roles, which can lead to burnout if not managed effectively. The pressure to continuously inspire and motivate others can be demanding and exhausting, potentially impacting the leader's well-being and long-term effectiveness.

Researchers are working on addressing these limitations to refine the theory further.

Servant Leadership:

Servant leadership is a model that emphasizes the leader's commitment to serving others and prioritizing their needs above their own. It was developed by Robert K. Greenleaf in the 1970s and first published in 1977 in an article dubbed “Essentials of Servant Leadership”. According to this theory, leaders should prioritize the needs of their team members, empower them, and help them grow both personally and professionally. By focusing on the well-being and development of their followers, servant leaders can create a culture of trust, loyalty, and motivation within an organization.

In church ministry, servant leaders focus on nurturing and supporting the spiritual well-being of their congregants. They exhibit humility, empathy, and a willingness to listen and understand the needs of others. By serving as role models, they encourage a culture of service and selflessness within the church community.

Whether in church or in a secular group, the successes of servant leadership lie in its ability to foster a positive work environment, enhance engagement and satisfaction among group members, and promote teamwork and collaboration.

In an article published in 1992, Larry C. Spears wrote that "Servant leadership seeks to involve others in decision making, is strongly based in ethical and caring behavior, and enhances the growth of workers while improving the caring and quality of organizational life."

Furthermore, Spears identified 10 servant leadership characteristics:

- Listening—a servant leader is committed to listening intently to others, and couples this with periods of reflection.
- Empathy—servant leaders make an effort to understand, empathize with, and accept others.
- Healing—servant leaders focus on helping others overcome emotional wounds and aid in their search for healing and wholeness.
- Awareness—servant leaders have both general and self-awareness, which contribute to an understanding of issues related to power, ethics, and values.

- Persuasion—in contrast to authoritarian leadership, servant leaders rely on convincing others based on the merit of arguments rather than on coercion or manipulation.
- Conceptualization—servant leaders are endowed with an ability to think beyond day-to-day realities and dream big.
- Foresight—servant leaders make deliberate efforts to "understand lessons from the past, the realities of the present, and the likely consequence of a decision for the future."
- Stewardship—servant leaders behave with the understanding that they have been entrusted with running the organization/team for the greater good of society.
- Commitment to the growth of people—servant leaders believe that people have an "intrinsic value beyond their intangible contributions as workers". This belief leads to a strong commitment to "the growth of each individual."
- Building community— servant leaders have a sincere desire to create true community within the organization and other institutions.

Despite the successes, servant leadership theory has also met some limitations such as:

- Some critics argue that it may not be suitable for all situations or industries, as it requires a certain level of trust and cooperation from followers.
- Some critics see the emphasis on serving others as a recipe to, sometimes, a lack of assertiveness or decision-making, which could hinder organizational efficiency.
- Furthermore, feminist scholars, including Pennsylvania State University professor emeritus Deborah Eicher-Catt, have noted that servant leadership theory is based on patriarchal approaches to leadership.
- Lastly, Brenda L.H. Marina and Debora Y. Fonteneau, in a 2012 article, point out that the servant leadership model and discourse has ignored the long history of Black servants

being subjugated and mistreated. Indeed, the term servant leadership may seem insensitive when applied to minority groups such as women, people of color, and others who have historically faced marginalization and mistreatment in the workplace and society at large.

In spite of these limitations, however, the theory of servant leadership offers a valuable perspective on leadership that prioritizes the needs of followers/members. The concept is also aligned to several Biblical teachings such as Jesus' command to "love others as you love yourself" and Evangelist Paul's imploration to "consider others as better than yourself."

Mathew 22:39 (NIV) And the second is like it: 'Love your neighbor as yourself.'

Philippians 2:3 (BLB) Do nothing out of selfish ambition or vain conceit, but in humility consider others better than yourselves.

Charismatic Leadership:

The theory of charismatic leadership was developed by Max Weber, a German sociologist, in the early 20th century. The theory is anchored on the belief that leaders can inspire and motivate their followers through their personal qualities and charisma.

According to Max Weber, charismatic leaders possess exceptional charm, confidence, and persuasive abilities, which enable them to influence and inspire others. This means that the successes of charismatic leadership lie in its ability to create a strong sense of vision and purpose among followers, through their attractive and strong personality (charisma).

Through personal charm, charisma, and persuasive communication skills, charismatic leaders usually have the power to rally people around a common goal, instill enthusiasm, and drive organizational change. They also often inspire loyalty and commitment, leading to increased follower engagement and performance.

In the context of church ministry, these leaders possess a strong presence and the ability to captivate and engage their congregants. They are good at the art of storytelling, use powerful speeches, and involve emotional appeals to motivate and mobilize the church community towards a shared vision.

Like the rest of the leadership models we have discussed, charismatic leadership also has its limitations. For example, there is a potential for over-reliance on the leader's personality and this may result in a lack of focus on long-term goals or the development of sustainable systems. In addition, charismatic leaders sometimes face challenges in maintaining their influence over time, as their charisma alone may not be sufficient to sustain long-term success.[1]

Authentic Leadership:

Authentic leadership is a contemporary leadership theory that emphasizes that it is important that leaders be genuine, self-aware, and transparent in their actions and interactions.

Although the concept of authenticity is not new, there has been a resurging interest in what constitutes authentic leadership as multiple researchers suggest that there may be much more to authentic leadership than just being true to oneself.

[1] Ref: Servant Leadership: A Journey into the Nature of Legitimate Power and Greatness 25th Anniversary Edition. Author - Greenleaf, Robert K.

A study done by Kate MacNeill, Ann Tonks, and Sarah Reynolds on co-leadership in the art industry identifies four characteristics that are crucial in authentic leadership. These include:

- Self-awareness - Goldman and Kernis (2002) described self-awareness as having an "awareness of, and trust in, one's motives, feelings, desires and self-relevant cognitions" (p. 18). They also emphasize that being able to identify one's strengths and weaknesses, being aware of one's emotions and trait characteristics, and having knowledge about one's behavior in particular circumstances are all indicative of self-awareness.
- Balanced processing - Balanced processing entails listening, consulting, and understanding beyond oneself. According to Kernis (2003) balanced processing relates to "not denying, distorting, exaggerating or ignoring private knowledge, internal experiences, and externally based evaluative information" (p. 14). In this case, self-awareness contributes substantially to one's capacity to practice balanced processing since knowledge of oneself automatically enhances a reflective approach to decision making.
- Relational transparency – Authentic leaders are unique in the sense that they share both their strengths and weaknesses with others. They not only share about their successes but also admit when they make mistakes and ask for forgiveness. This sharing of their feelings and motives enables authentic leaders to break any emotional wall built by their followers/members, building strong authentic relationships with them.
- Internalized moral perspective – Authentic leaders have an internalized moral perspective that guides them and helps regulate their behavior. They have strong moral values that they abide by as they serve their team/organization.

In the context of church ministry, this theory focuses on leaders who lead with integrity, aligning their values and beliefs with their actions. Authentic leaders in church ministry strive to build trust, foster meaningful relationships, and inspire others through their genuine commitment to serving the congregation and community.[2]

Adaptive Leadership:

Adaptive leadership is a model that recognizes the need for leaders to navigate and address complex challenges and changes within an organization or community. In church ministry, adaptive leadership involves leaders who are able to adapt and respond to the evolving needs and dynamics of the congregation and the broader society. They encourage innovation, promote learning, and mobilize the church community to effectively address issues and seize opportunities for growth and transformation.

Biblical Perspectives on Leadership

In this topic, we will delve into the biblical principles of leadership and see examples of godly leadership found in the Bible, highlighting how they can be applied to church ministry.

To shed light on some biblical principles of leadership, let us consider the following verses.

---

[2] Reference: Authentic Leadership: Development and Validation of a Theory-Based Measure Authors: Fred O. Walumbwa, Bruce J. Avolio, William L. Gardner, Tara S. Wernsing, Suzanne J. Peterson © 2008 Southern Management Association, published by SAGE Publications

1st Peter 5:1-4

To the elders among you, I appeal as a fellow elder and a witness of Christ's sufferings who also will share in the glory to be revealed: 2 Be shepherds of God's flock that is under your care, watching over them—not because you must, but because you are willing, as God wants you to be; not pursuing dishonest gain, but eager to serve; 3 not lording it over those entrusted to you, but being examples to the flock. 4 And when the Chief Shepherd appears, you will receive the crown of glory that will never fade away.

Matthew 20:26–28

It shall not be so among you. But whoever would be great among you must be your servant, and whoever would be first among you must be your slave, even as the Son of Man came not to be served but to serve, and to give his life as a ransom for many.

Luke 12:48

To whom much is given, much is expected.

John 13:13–17

You call me Teacher and Lord, and you are right, for so I am. If I then, your Lord and Teacher, have washed your feet, you also ought to wash one another's feet. For I have given you an example, that you also should do just as I have done to you. Truly, truly, I say to you, a servant is not greater than his master, nor is a messenger greater than the one who sent him. If you know these things, blessed are you if you do them.

2 Corinthians 3:5

It is not that we think we are qualified to do anything on our own. Our qualification comes from God.

According to scriptures, biblical godly leadership is based on:

1. Willingness to serve –biblical leadership is built on the principle that, like every other part of our lives, a leader must surrender their leadership skills for God's use in the church. Leaders in church should do it willingly and not because they must.
2. Humility – church leaders should remain humble and desire to serve more than to be served just as Jesus demonstrated when he washed the disciples' feet.
3. Have an unselfish/selfless motive – bible-based leaderships call for a selfless attitude that does not seek to wrongfully gain from the position. The goal of leadership must be beyond and larger than SELF. Instead, biblical leaders understand that their reward is the crown of glory that will never fade away.
4. Be an example – Peter implores elders to be examples to the flock and lord it over them. Leaders must model godliness and lead from the front instead of issuing directions and rules that they themselves are not following.
5. Accountability – leaders must realize that they are ultimately answerable to the owner of their lives, skills, charisma, and personalities. As such, they are stewards of God's grace and must work to see that the grace of God id not in vain or misused in the church.
6. Reliance on God – Church leaders must rely on God for wisdom and grace to lead the church. They must always remember that Jesus is the chief Shepherd and the owner and keeper of the church. As such, His will and direction must be followed as the leader (through the Holy Spirit) guide and cheer the church on.

7. Responsibility [3]

Leadership in the Bible

Examples of Good leaders

Jesus Christ

Jesus' leadership saw the transformation of mere men into noble servant of God who led the establishment of the church and the sharing of the gospel, as directed in the Great Commission.

Acts 4:13

When they saw the courage of Peter and John and realized that they were unschooled, ordinary men, they were astonished, and they took note that these men had been with Jesus.

The transformation happened because, as a great leader, Jesus took his time to teach and train the disciples. He would retreat with them for teaching and prayer as a way to empower them for the task ahead.

Thirdly, Jesus prayed for his disciples and other believers – that they may be strengthened and established by God. He had their/our interest at heart.

---

[3] Biblical Perspectives on Leadership and Organizations by J. Lee Whittington · 2016

Biblical organizational leadership: Principles from the life of Jesus in the Gospel of John by Craig A. Bell, Christa M. Bonnet, Stuart W. Boyer, W. David Winner, Debra Jean, Kenneth Dixon, Joshua Henson,

Matthew 26:31–35; Mark 14:27–31; John 13:36–38)

"Simon, Simon, Satan has asked to sift each of you like wheat. But I have prayed for you, Simon, that your faith will not fail. And when you have turned back, strengthen your brothers."

John 17:17-24

"Sanctify them by[d] the truth; your word is truth. 18 As you sent me into the world, I have sent them into the world. 19 For them I sanctify myself, that they too may be truly sanctified.

My prayer is not for them alone. I pray also for those who will believe in me through their message, that all of them may be one, Father, just as you are in me, and I am in you. May they also be in us so that the world may believe that you have sent me. I have given them the glory that you gave me, that they may be one as we are one— I in them and you in me—so that they may be brought to complete unity. Then the world will know that you sent me and have loved them even as you have loved me.

Father, I want those you have given me to be with me where I am, and to see my glory, the glory you have given me because you loved me before the creation of the world."

Prophet Deborah

Deborah was the only Female Judge in the history of Israel. As a judge, she exhibited great courage and faith in God when she led the children of Israel to war against xxx. Her passion and zeal for her community enabled her to encourage, motivate, and lead the children of Israel in war.

She is a great example of the fact that godly leaders do not think selfishly but rather, build up a community among the people of God.

Prophet Samuel

Samuel led the children of Israel as a prophet for a long time, being a voice of reason and guiding them and their leaders. He constantly consulted with God and was faithful till the very end.

When he had chosen and anointed King Saul as instructed by God, prophet Samuel welcomes a public review of his service to the people. This shows that he was a man of great integrity and did not take advantage of his position and oppress the people.

1 Samuel 12:3

Here I stand. Testify against me in the presence of the LORD and his anointed. Whose ox have I taken? Whose donkey have I taken? Whom have I cheated? Whom have I oppressed? From whose hand have I accepted a bribe to make me shut my eyes? If I have done any of these things, I will make it right."

Moses

Moses chose his identify as an Israelite and foregone the privileges of living as Pharaoh's family.

Hebrews 11:24-28 (NIV)

By faith Moses, when he had grown up, refused to be known as the son of Pharaoh's daughter. He chose to be mistreated along with the people of God rather than to enjoy the fleeting pleasures of sin. He regarded disgrace for the sake of Christ as of greater value than the treasures of Egypt, because he was looking ahead to his reward. By faith he left Egypt, not fearing the king's anger; he persevered because he saw him who is invisible. By faith he kept the Passover and the application of blood, so that the destroyer of the firstborn would not touch the firstborn of Israel.

Secondly, Moses was humble and ready to receive advice. As advised by his father-in-law, he chose twelve leaders from the twelve tribes of Israel to help him lead the people.

Exodus 18:19-25

Listen now to me and I will give you some advice, and may God be with you. You must be the people's representative before God and bring their disputes to him. 20 Teach them his decrees and instructions, and show them the way they are to live and how they are to behave. 21 But select capable men from all the people—men who fear God, trustworthy men who hate dishonest gain—and appoint them as officials over thousands, hundreds, fifties and tens. 22 Have them serve as judges for the people at all times, but have them bring every difficult case to you; the simple cases they can decide themselves. That will make your load lighter, because they will share it with you. 23 If you do this and God so commands, you will be able to stand the strain, and all these people will go home satisfied."

24 Moses listened to his father-in-law and did everything he said. 25 He chose capable men from all Israel and made them leaders of the people, officials over thousands, hundreds, fifties and tens.

Numbers 12:3

Now Moses was a very humble man, more humble than anyone else on the face of the earth.

Thirdly, Moses was selfless and thought about God's praise and the Israelites' plight. When faced with the suggestion that the children of Israel be destroyed and God makes a greater nation from him, he interceded for 40 days and nights. His response sought to protect God's reputation as a promise keeper.

Deuteronomy 9:26-29

"And I prayed to the LORD and said, "O Lord GOD, do not destroy Your people, Your inheritance, whom You redeemed through Your greatness and brought out of Egypt with a mighty hand. Remember Your servants Abraham, Isaac, and Jacob. Overlook the stubbornness of this people and the wickedness of their sin. Otherwise, those in the land from which You brought us out will say, 'Because the LORD was not able to bring them into the land He had promised them, and because He hated them, He has brought them out to kill them in the wilderness.' But they are Your people, Your inheritance, whom You brought out by Your great power and outstretched arm."

Fourthly, Moses empowered other leaders amongst the Israelites. He worked with the likes of Aaron, Joshua, and Caleb among the many leaders chosen as officials over thousands, hundreds, fifties and tens.

Lastly, Moses was consistent and did not turn away from God over the course of the many years of his service. For over 40 years, he led the Israelites reminding them of God's promise and teaching them of God's laws.

Queen Esther

As the queen in a foreign land, Esther fought for the rights of the Jews who were foreigners in the land and were being wrongfully targeted by Herman. Like Moses, she sacrificially chose to attend to the plight of her people and not hide behind the success/positioning that she had as a queen.

In her dealings, she relied on God through fasting and prayer. As a result, she acted with courage and faced the king to petition for Jews.

Esther 4:16 *I will go to the king, even though it is against the law. And if I perish, I perish.*

Esther was also humble and teachable, and she listened to her adopted father Mordecai and the counsel of the head eunuch Hegai. Her humility and wisdom earned her favor everywhere she went, including before the king.

Examples of bad leadership

King Saul

Chosen by the people to be king, Saul began as a humble king that God anointed through prophet Saul. However, he turned against the Lord, displeasing and dishonouring Him in his service. For example, he becomes impatient and sacrifices instead of waiting for prophet Samuel.

He had attributes such as disobedience, jealousy, ignoring godly counsel, and resenting those who challenged his unreasonable emotions and misinformed judgments.

King Nebuchadnezzar

Nebuchadnezzar had great success but ended up in an arrogant boast about his abilities and majesty. In response, God caused him to be reduced to a grass-eating animal. It is a good thing that he repented and acknowledged God and was restored as king of Babylon.

From Nebuchadnezzar, we are reminded that leaders must remain humble toward God regardless of the achievements and successes they have over their service.

Daniel 4:29-33

29 At the end of the twelve months he was walking about the royal palace of Babylon. 30 The king spoke, saying, "Is not this great Babylon, that I have built for a royal dwelling by my mighty power and for the honor of my majesty?"

31 While the word was still in the king's mouth, pa voice fell from heaven: "King Nebuchadnezzar, to you it is spoken: the kingdom has departed from you! 32 And they shall drive you from men, and your dwelling shall be with the beasts of the field. They shall make you eat grass like oxen; and seven 1times shall pass over you, until you know that the Most High rules in the kingdom of men, and gives it to whomever He chooses."

33 That very hour the word was fulfilled concerning Nebuchadnezzar; he was driven from men and ate grass like oxen; his body was wet with the dew of heaven till his hair had grown like eagles' feathers and his nails like birds' claws.[4]

Leadership Development and Training

The question of whether leadership is made or born has been ongoing for a long time. From a biblical perspective, however, we see a beautiful balance of divine choice and training upon leaders in the bible. Considering the examples of leaders like Moses, David, Joseph, and the

---

[4] Reflection on the leadership practice of Saul as a failure of leadership for church pastors by D. Ming Department of Geological Studies, Sekolah Tinggi Teologia Kadesi,Yogyakarta,Indonesia. E-mail: davidmingming3@gmail.com; ORCID:https://orcid.org/0000-0001-9649-1622

disciples, we see God choosing these individuals as leaders among his people and taking them through training and disciplining to empower and enable them to serve.

David was anointed to be king but served as a shepherd of his father's flocks in the wilderness. It is through his shepherding experience that God trained David through fighting and killing the bear and the lion that had tried to attack his sheep. This experience prepared him to fight against Goliath and lead Israel's army to overcome their enemies over the course of his leadership.

Moses was also trained in the wilderness for 40 years before he was officially commissioned through the encounter at the burning bush. He would lead the children of Israel across the desert in their journey from Egypt to the promised land. Equally, Joseph went through betrayal, slavery, and imprisonment before being appointed as second to the king of Egypt (Pharaoh).

For all these leaders, it was important that they should remain focused on God and go through the training for effective ministries and leadership afterward.

In the secular world, leadership training has also been identified as a key tool to position individuals for team leader and executive positions in various organizations. The training takes various shapes such as direct mentorship, training sessions, and higher education among others.

In the same way, the church should embrace and adopt strategies and programs necessary for developing and training leaders within the church. This can be achieved through:

- Mentoring - senior leadership should share with upcoming leaders.
- Educational programs – churches should embrace godly training programs that explore the traits of great leadership.
- Create leadership opportunities within various ministries and allow several people to minister and lead while you oversee the ministry.

- Offer internship opportunities to upcoming ministers and leaders to allow them learn hands-on skills in ministry.
- Bible study – study leadership models and examples in the bible as an individual and as a team of leaders within the church.

Ethical Leadership in Church Ministry

As hinted in the models of leadership, ethics and values in leadership is a topic of contention. This is the case both in the secular world as well as in the church ministry. There are various ethical challenges faced by leaders in the context of church ministry, and these have become even more transparent in this generation where stories of false ministers of the gospel fill the social media platforms across the world.

The greatest two contemporary ethical issues relating to church leadership these days are **deceit** and ***manipulation***.

Thes two work together and manifest when church leaders use the word of God or their positions as ministers to deceive and manipulate their congregants toward doing things that will benefit them as individuals. These include tactics such as conning people into giving their entire possessions to the minister, leaving their families to serve the minister/church, and as witnessed in Shakahola, neglect their bodies and lives in an ungodly non-biblical way.

It is important to emphasize the importance of integrity, accountability, and moral decision-making among church leaders since they are answerable to God himself and Jesus, the chief shepherd. Church leaders must be transparent and without greed like Prophet Samuel modeled.

They must give themselves to the service of God with a sincere and pure heart for God to walk with them and give them good success.

1 Corinthians 4:2 *Now it is required that those who have been given a trust must prove faithful.*

Matthew 6:24 *No one can serve two masters. Either you will hate the one and love the other, or you will be devoted to the one and despise the other. You cannot serve both God and money.*

James 3:1 *Not many of you should become teachers, my fellow believers, because you know that we who teach will be judged more strictly.*

Leadership and Conflict Resolution in Church Settings

This topic should focus on strategies for resolving conflicts and promoting reconciliation within the church, emphasizing the role of leaders in facilitating healthy dialogue and fostering unity.

The church ministry and leadership may have to deal with conflict on three levels:

- Conflict between leaders - Leadership positions appear enviable and the desire to lead may lead to conflict eruption.
- Conflict within the congregation - conflict is bound to occur wherever there are human interactions - including in the church - just like in any other organization.
- Conflict between the church and the community around them.

Church leaders have the responsibility to create an environment that will prevent and minimize conflict and resolve any conflict that arises amongst the fellow leaders, congregants, and the community at large. Everything rises from and falls on leadership (Maxwell, 1993).

Leaders should approach conflict resolution based on a theology of reconciliation to enrich the practice of negotiation and mediation by placing them within the spectrum of God's actions in the world.

Theoretical and practical presuppositions regarding conflict resolution have been examined in the work of three major theorists, namely John Burton, Roger Fisher and Dudley Weeks. The study of their theories and practices of conflict resolution reveals that they preferred different approaches or made divergent theoretical points of departure. Christian leaders should study such models and adopt them or a cocktail of two or three of them as deemed effective in their circumstance.

Examples of Methods of conflict resolution to consider.

Theology of mediation

The Christian theology of mediation has its source in the mediation between God and humanity through the person of Jesus Christ the Mediator. An analysis of Jesus Christ's role as Mediator therefore provides the foundation for a theology of mediation and elucidates the relation between mediation and conflict resolution in theological terms.

If the mediation of Jesus Christ through the cross and resurrection makes reconciliation with God and between persons possible, are we at liberty to conclude that as the Mediator Jesus Christ was 'doing conflict resolution'? Certainly, he was resolving the conflict in the form of alienation between God and humanity caused by humanity's selfishness, egocentricity and rejection of God. Jesus' mediation through his life, death and resurrection met the needs of God and of humanity so that the way was opened for the restoration of humanity's future relationship with God.

As followers and models of Jesus Christ, therefore, church leaders should take up the ministry of reconciliation – connecting the people to God and to each other through preaching forgiveness and its power to:

- acknowledges the fact that we all sometimes fall short of the best we can do, that we are all still growing and improving.
- communicates to conflict partners that they are not being defined or judged solely on some past negative behaviour.
- reaches for the positive power of the conflict partner to learn from the past and make positive contributions in spite of past behaviour that has helped create and perpetuate damaging conflicts.
- helps create an atmosphere that encourages both conflict partners to move beyond the past and focus on the present-future.
- increases the positive power of the person doing the forgiving. (Weeks 1992:181)

Arbitration

In arbitration, a neutral third party serves as a judge who is responsible for resolving the dispute. An example in the bible is the story of the two women who both wanted to take the live baby in 1 Kings 3:16-28.

16 Now two prostitutes came to the king and stood before him. 17 One of them said, Pardon me, my lord. This woman and I live in the same house, and I had a baby while she was there with me. 18 The third day after my child was born, this woman also had a baby. We were alone; there was no one in the house but the two of us. 19 During the night this woman's son died because she lay on him. 20 So she got up in the middle of the night and took my son from my side while I your servant was asleep. She put him by her breast and put her dead son by my breast. 21 The next morning, I got up to nurse my son-and he was dead! But when I looked at him closely in the morning light, I saw that it wasn't the son I had borne."22 The other woman said, No! The living one is my son; the dead one is yours."But the first one insisted, No! The dead one is yours; the living one is mine."And so they argued before the king. 23 The king said, This one says, 'My son is alive and your son is dead,' while that one says, 'No! Your son is dead and mine is alive.' "24 Then the king said, Bring me a sword."So they brought a sword for the king. 25 He then gave an order: Cut the living child in two and give half to one and half to the other."26 The woman whose son was alive was deeply moved out of love for her son and said to the king, Please, my lord, give her the living baby! Don't kill him!"But the other said, Neither I nor you shall have him. Cut him in two!"27 Then the king gave his ruling: Give the living baby to the first woman. Do not kill him; she is his mother."28 When all Israel heard the verdict the king had given, they held the king in awe, because they saw that he had wisdom from God to administer justice.

Since the arbitrator listens as each side argues its case and presents relevant evidence, then renders a binding decision, he/she must be neutral and just. It also important that both parties should highly respect and be willing to take the decision made by the arbitrators. This is because an arbitrator's decisions are usually confidential and cannot be appealed.

Negotiation

This is the most basic means of settling differences and resolving conflicts between any parties. It includes having back-and-forth communication between the parties involved in conflict with the goal of trying to reach an agreeable solution. A negotiated agreement can become a contract and be enforceable.

Some characteristics of Negotiation include:

- Voluntary
- Private and confidential
- Quick and inexpensive
- Informal and unstructured
- Parties control the process, make their own decisions and reach their own agreements (there is no third-party decision maker)
- Can result in a win-win solution

As example in the bible, and one of the earliest negotiation sessions in recorded history is found in the Bible, Chapter 18 of Genesis, where Abraham negotiates with God regarding the destruction of the twin cities of Sodom and Gomorrah. Although Abraham was not directly involved in the conflict/strained relationship, he wanted to negotiate for God not to destroy the two cities.

To ensure that conflicts are prevented and resolved within church ministry, leaders should consider the following tactics:

- Set a Good Example by Modeling Christ. Leaders should not be a cause of conflict or disunity and should seek to resolve any issues between them and other leaders or members of fellowship.
- Directly talk to the church against division and the importance of resolving any conflicts and walk in unity. Care should be taken not to make someone specific feel inferior in front of the group or embarrassed inadvertently. Speaking to issues allow the leader to speak to key issues broadly and reaffirm the values that the church stand for.

- Weave relational wisdom into your church – this is a gospel-driven form of emotional intelligence that helps people to not think of conflict in two dimension- me against you. Instead, relationships are viewed as "three-dimensionally" by seeking to be God-aware, self-aware and other-aware in every relational interaction. Relational wisdom reminds those involved in conflict that which Jesus taught when He commanded us to "love God with all our hearts and to love our neighbors as we love ourselves" (Matt. 22:37-40).
- Work patiently with people as they process their emotions and experiences – Since people always interpret our words and actions through a filter of their own life experiences and emotions, a seemingly innocent statement in a sermon or conversation can trigger an intense emotional reaction in others. It is important that church leaders understand the background of congregants and help them in the journey to healing and wholeness.
- Diffuse explosive meetings with a six part format – Ken Sande's article suggests a six part format to help turn volatile meetings into a time of humble self-examination and constructive problem solving. The format emphasizes that everyone who speaks should be expected to summarize the issue to be discussed through the six-part format:
    - Briefly stated, how do you feel because of this problem?
    - Which fruit of the Spirit are you seeking to display as you speak today (Gal. 5:22-23: "love, joy, peace, patience, kindness, goodness, faithfulness, gentleness, self-control")?
    - What have you done that might have contributed to this problem?
    - What do you think would please God as we work through this situation?
    - What steps have you already taken to make things better?
    - What are you now willing to do to help resolve this problem?

- What do you suggest others do to help resolve this problem?

- Cultivate community through teambuilding activities among congregants. This helps to break the ice, create empathy, build friendships, and ultimately, make it easier for people to resolves any issues and maintain peace.[5]

---

[5] The journal of Applied Christian Leadership (ISSN 1933-3978, 1933-3986) Vol 15

Conflict Management across Cultures: Pathways and Patterns by Augsburger, David. Louisville:John Knox Press, 1992.

Leadership Journal 9 "How Can I Keep From Wearing Out?" by Dowing, Gary W. (1988): 27-31.

Leadership and diversity in church ministry.

Diversity is, basically, variety. In recent times, the word diversity has taken on the specific connotation of "variety of people within a group"—the differences among the people being racial, cultural, gender-based, etc. Diversity was God's idea. Even a cursory study of science reveals an amazing variety of plant and animal life. People, God's final creation, are diverse, too. He did not create us as clones or robots. He created two different genders (Mark 10:6). The creation of male and female is diversity at its most basic—the sexes are very different, yet complementary.

Another act of God that created diversity occurred at the Tower of Babel (Genesis 11:9). Humankind was clustered together, and God wanted them to "be fruitful and multiply and fill the earth" (Genesis 9:1). To expedite their obedience, He confused their languages, making it impossible for them to work together. From there, humanity spread out across the earth, and people with the same language remained together. Over time, cultures, races, and regional dialects emerged and resulted in the diversity we now know.

Diversity is part of being human. God delights in the plethora of differences His human creatures possess. The book of Revelation describes the final gathering of God's people from "every nation, tribe, and tongue" (Revelation 7:9). The angels and elders around God's throne adore Jesus with the words "with your blood you purchased for God persons from every tribe and language and people and nation" (Revelation 5:9). So God enjoys the diversity within the human race. We are each created in His image for His pleasure and glory (Revelation 4:11; Colossians 1:16). He designed us the way we are and delights in His handiwork (Psalm 139:13–16).

However, in our modern culture, the focus on diversity can become its own god. Diversity itself is revered rather than the One who created that diversity. An emphasis on diversity tends to highlight our differences. God is more concerned with unity (Ephesians 4:3). Galatians 3:28 says, “There is neither Jew nor Gentile, neither slave nor free, nor is there male and female, for you are all one in Christ Jesus.” God is saying that our differences are not what should define the children of God. Those who belong to the Lord Jesus should first define themselves as God’s children. We must be willing to set diversity aside in favor of unity in spirit. Jesus’ passionate prayer in John 17 shows that His desire for His disciples was that “they may be one as you and I are one” (verse 22).

So, what does it mean to be “one”? When we are born again (John 3:3), we are created anew in Christ Jesus. Our fleshly differences become secondary to our new nature in Christ. We are unified around the centrality of God’s Word. We have “one Lord, one faith, one baptism” (Ephesians 4:5). Regardless of racial, cultural, or gender differences, God’s children hold to His Word as their final authority on all matters, including cultural and social issues. Some try to use “diversity” as an excuse to justify immorality or homosexuality (1 Corinthians 6:9). While we all have different sin strongholds, we cannot allow unrepentant sin to continue under the guise of diversity. The diversity God created is good; sin can indeed be diverse, but God has nothing to do with it.

Human differences such as race, temperament, and culture are to be celebrated, tolerated, and incorporated in our goal of being “one” in Christ (John 17:20–23). However, when diversity is made into an idol, we become self-centered and divisive. When every difference is treated as sacred, selfishness rules and oneness is sacrificed in favor of individual preference. When we exalt our preferences over unity, we become demanding and proud, rather than selfless and forgiving (Ephesians 4:32; Philippians 2:4). John 17:23 encapsulates the desire of Jesus for all His children. In this last, long, recorded prayer before His crucifixion, Jesus prayed, “I in them and you in me—so that they may be brought to complete unity. Then the world will know that you sent me and have loved them even as you have loved me." While we can and should appreciate the value of the various nuances of being human, our goal must always be to become more like Jesus (Romans 8:29).[6]

[6] Got Question.org

The need for loyalty.

Allegiance is a vital component for each leader. The Bible is the clear, "You shall reap what you sow." You can never rise in leadership when your integrity is compromised, when it comes to your loyalty to the leaders above you. God saw it valuable to incorporate loyalty in the making of covenants with His people. In Deuteronomy 7:9, we see this vital component, it says, "Therefore know that the LORD your God, He is God, the faithful God who keeps covenant and mercy for a thousand generations with those who love Him and keep His commandments."

In the fulfillment of the covenant, God requires that man should be loyal and the consequences for disloyalty cannot be abated, as disloyalty shows that you do not belong to Him. God says in Deuteronomy 8:19, "Then it shall be, if you by any means forget the LORD your God, and follow other gods, and serve them and worship them, I testify against you this day that you shall surely perish." Likewise, as we imitate God, we are also supposed to be faithful in leadership. To the leaders above us, to the call upon our lives and to the people we are leading.

Paul speaks of his "loyal companion" in Philippians 4:3 who probably labored with Paul. Burdett Hart a clergyman of New Britain Church says this about loyalty, "Loyalty that will do anything, that will endure anything, that will make the whole being consecrate to Him, is what Christ wants. Anything else is not worthy of Him." In leadership, you need to be faithful and loyal, because the Chief Shepherd and the Bishop of our souls will come with payment for each and every one and will pay accordingly.

An embodiment of loyalty is demonstrated through and through by Ruth in her devotion and duty to her mother-in-law. Ruth lived in the times of the judges and was "of the women of Moab." She was married to a son of an Israelite while they were living in the land of Moab. Sometimes later, her father-in-law, her brother-in-law and her husband all died. Ruth had to make a decision whether to remain behind amongst her people or follow Naomi back to Judah, a land she had never known. Her loyalty and love towards he mother-in-law Naomi is expressed by her commitment for Naomi. In Ruth 1:16 she says, "Entreat me not to leave you, or to turn back from following after you; for wherever you go, I will go; and wherever you lodge, I will lodge; your people shall be my people, and your God, my God."

Do not allow the Orpah kind of leadership to overpower you, "Orpah kissed her mother-in-law goodbye." The Ruth kind of leadership is one full of loyalty, she chose the path of loyalty even if it meant giving up everything she was used to in Moab. Many people in leadership bequeath their roles and other pull down their leaders when a new opportunity arises. This is Orpah kind of leadership that is full of disloyalty.

Faithfulness is always rewarded. In the conquest of the fortified city of Jericho, Joshua sent two spies to look over the land. A heroine of the Old Testament is introduced to us by the name Rahab. She was a prostitute in the city of Jericho, when the two spies stayed in her home and she protected them. She helped them to escape, provided that she and her family would be spared in the coming battle. Through her faithfulness, though the city was completely destroyed, every man, woman and child in it was killed, only Rahab and her family were spared.

Rahab is in the lineage of Jesus Christ, she married Salmon from the tribe of Judah, and her son was Boaz. Boaz became the husband of Ruth who is Joseph's legal father of Jesus is her direct descendant. Her faithfulness is greatly rewarded despite her past history; her intelligence and the skill of having good information are qualities that that should be emulated by all leaders. Just like Rahab, leaders who are committed faithfully their actions will always gain rewards that might outlive them.

David’s mighty men also referred to as the “thirty chiefs” are a group proved their faithfulness and loyalty to their leader. They were the toughest military warriors in David’s army who were credited with heroic feats. They had considerable military skills and the blessing of God who served an import role in protecting the king and fighting for Israel’s freedom.

Among the thirty, Josheb-basshebeth killed eight hundred men in one battle using only his spear, Eleazar had stayed on the battlefield when other soldiers fled and he killed so many Philistines until his hand was stuck clenched around his hand. Another notable action was performed by Abishai, the leader of the mighty men who killed three hundred men with a spear. Among the group, these three stood out, Josheb-basshebeth, Eleazar and Shammah who at Lehi took stand and killed many Philistines.

When David desired water from well that was in Bethlehem, three of the might men knew about his desire. Though at the gate of the city were soldiers guarding the city, the three broke through the soldiers and went to bring David water so that he may quench his thirst. At this particular time Saul and his army were looking for David.

When the water was brought to David, he would not drink it for they had put their lives at risk just to bring him the water. This act, shows that they were faithful soldiers and loyal to their master. There are several lesson we can learn from their act that exhibit character of faithfulness in leadership.

Every faithful leader covets to understand the desired goal. Actively listening, observing and looking for way of success toward the goal. David’s men understood what needed to be done. Many people in leadership sometimes do not know what is needed to be done and are unaware of their place. This many times makes the church to stagnate and not realize the expected desires.

Secondly, faithful leaders take responsibility and are willingly to follow through. Jesus gave a parable of a faithful servant and said that blessed of the servant who will be found doing what is expected of them. But, when the servant become gluttonous and misuses his position will be cut in half and his portion shall be given to another. “And that servant who knew his master's will, and did not prepare himself or do according to his will, shall be beaten with many stripes. But he who did not know, yet committed things deserving of stripes, shall be beaten with few. For everyone to whom much is given, from him much will be required; and to whom much has been committed, of him they will ask the more.” Luke 12:47-48.

When a child is born, the child has no responsibilities bestowed on them – everything that is needed by them is done. As the years advance, we take on more responsibilities and learn that responsibility has rewards and irresponsibility has less desired outcome. The law emphasizes the responsibility of individuals to respond in morally appropriate ways. The standard is the same for all leaders.

Also, every faithful leader is flexible and can adapt depending on the needs at a particular season. Inflexibility delays results and we know that a kings business requires haste. As Saul was out to kill David, David became flexible when the priest inquired why he was by himself. He makes up a story to appease the inquisitive priest, in 1 Samuel 21:8 he says, “And David said to Ahimelech, "Is there not here on hand a spear or a sword? For I have brought neither my sword nor my weapons with me, because the king's business required haste."

Other characteristic of faithful leaders are having an optimistic attitude, can be counted to follow through with promises made, are trustworthy and they understand that they are not all knowing and are willing to collaborate with others.

Bibliography

The journal of Applied Christian Leadership (ISSN 1933-3978, 1933-3986) Vol 15

Augsburger, David. Conflict Management across Cultures: Pathways and Patterns Louisville:John Knox Press, 1992.

Dowing, Gary W. Leadership Journal 9 "How Can I Keep From Wearing Out?" (1988): 27-31.

D. Ming Department of Geological Studies, Reflection on the leadership practice of Saul as a failure of leadership for church pastors. Sekolah Tinggi Teologia Kadesi,Yogyakarta,Indonesia. E-mail: davidmingming3@gmail.com; ORCID:https://orcid.org/0000-0001-9649-1622

J. Lee Whittington · 2016. Biblical Perspectives on Leadership and Organizations by

Craig A. Bell, Christa M. Bonnet, Stuart W. Boyer, W. David Winner, Debra Jean, Kenneth Dixon, Joshua Henson, Biblical organizational leadership: Principles from the life of Jesus in the Gospel of John.

Fred O. Walumbwa, Bruce J. Avolio, William L. Gardner, Tara S. Wernsing, Suzanne J. Peterson. Authentic Leadership: Development and Validation of a Theory-Based Measure. © 2008 Southern Management Association, published by SAGE Publications

MIX
Papier aus verantwortungsvollen Quellen
Paper from responsible sources
FSC® C105338

Printed by Books on Demand GmbH, Norderstedt / Germany